High Win Rate Scalping Setups

Advanced High Win Rate Scalping Strategies for Trading Crypto, Forex and Stocks in 2023!

Table of Contents

Introduction

In this book, we will explore various profitable scalping strategies that utilize technical indicators, machine learning, and artificial intelligence to achieve high win rates in your trades. In this book you will learn advanced scalping concepts that will allow you to make massive gains in the market and take your trading to the next level.

Why Scalping?

Scalping is particularly well-suited for the volatile and dynamic nature of the cryptocurrency markets, offering numerous trading opportunities throughout the day.

Here are a few reasons why scalping is a great way to trade the markets:

- *Compounding gains:* Successful scalpers can rapidly accumulate profits by executing multiple trades per day, taking advantage of the power of compounding.

- *Can make hundreds in minutes:* With the right strategy, scalpers can capitalize on numerous trading opportunities and potentially make significant gains in a matter of minutes.

- *Reduced market exposure:* Scalping allows traders to be in and out of the market quickly, minimizing the impact of sudden adverse price movements.

- *Make money in bull and bear markets:* Scalping enables traders to make money regardless of market direction, as they can take advantage of price fluctuations in both rising and falling markets.

Who is this Book for?

- Traders who are already familiar with the basics of trading and are looking to expand their knowledge on scalping strategies

- Experienced scalpers seeking new ideas and advanced techniques to improve their win rate

- Anyone interested in learning about high win rate scalping setups and how to implement them in their trading routine

By the end of this book, you will have a deep understanding of the various components that contribute to high win rate scalping setups. You'll be equipped with the knowledge and skills necessary to create and optimize your own scalping strategies, ultimately leading to consistent and profitable results in your trading journey.

Now let's get started!

Chapter 1: The Core Principles of Profitable Scalping

Scalping is a fast-paced and high-frequency trading technique that aims to capitalize on small price movements in the market. To successfully implement a scalping strategy, traders must adhere to a set of fundamental principles that serve as the foundation for consistent and lucrative trading.

These core principles include:

- Use a Mechanical Rule Based Strategy: Implement a systematic approach to trading that removes emotions and subjectivity from decision-making, ensuring consistency in execution.

- Use a Strategy that is proven to Work: Utilize a trading strategy that you have backtested on historical data and has been shown to be profitable based on the backtest statistics.

- Analyze Market Conditions: You need to continuously monitor and assess market conditions. Identify the market direction (is it up, down or sideways?) and choose a scalping strategy that will work best in the current market conditions.

- Use Risk Management and Dynamic Stop Losses: Set appropriate stop losses, position sizes, and risk-reward ratios to protect your capital and maximize your gains.

  Dynamic stop losses such as the Parabolic SAR or the Average True Range are a great way to catch larger market moves, while effectively managing risk.

By mastering these core principles, traders can enhance their scalping performance and increase the likelihood of achieving profitability in their trading endeavors. In the following chapters, we will delve into various aspects of scalping, including specific strategies, indicators, and optimization techniques, to further refine your scalping skills and maximize your profits.

Now let's take a look at an example of how a profitable scalping strategy looks in action, and analyze the components in more detail.

Example: DOGE/USDT VWAP Scalping Strategy

In this example we will look at a simple yet profitable scalping strategy I created myself on the charting platform TradingView.

This is a mean reversion strategy for trading Doge/USDT on the 1 minute timeframe and uses only three indicators:

- VWAP (volume weighted average price)

- ADX (average directional index)

- RSI – Length set to 4

How this strategy works:

- The VWAP will act like a magnet for price, when price rises above or below it is likely to revert back to it at some point.

- The RSI is used for identifying entry signals to pinpoint when price is likely to revert back to the VWAP.

- This strategy is designed for sideways market conditions, and uses the ADX to filter for these conditions.

As you can see, this is a very simple strategy, now let's take a look at the backtest statistics for this particular strategy, including the win rate and profitability.

Backtest statistics of this strategy:

- This strategy has a 62.75% win rate

- A profit factor of 2.15 (very good)

- It made **$4877** from a $10,000 account over the course of **two weeks** (not using leverage)

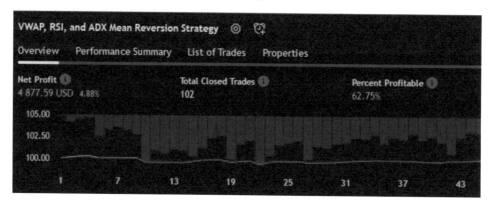

The net profit and win rate of this strategy

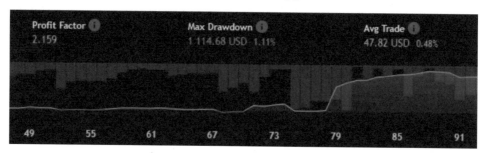

The profit factor and max draw down of this strategy

Next we'll take a look at the entry and exit rules for this scalping strategy.

Long conditions:

The following rules must be met in order to execute a long trade:

- The ADX is below 25 indicating a sideways market

- Price is below the VWAP

- Enter long when the RSI crosses **above 70** (overbought)

- Exit long when the RSI crosses below 30 (oversold)

- The stop loss is set at 5%, and take profit 15%

Short conditions:

The following rules must be met in order to execute a short trade:

- The ADX is below 25 indicating a sideways market

- Price is above the VWAP

- Enter short when the RSI crosses **below 30** (oversold)

- Exit short when the RSI crosses above 70 (overbought)

- The stop loss is set at 5%, and take profit 15%

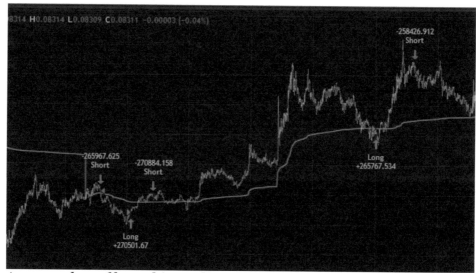

A screenshot of how this trading strategy looks in action

What Makes this a Profitable Scalping Strategy?

The reason why this strategy is so profitable is the combination of these indicators and how each of them plays a specific role to create a robust trading strategy.

Here is a breakdown of how exactly each indicator is used in this strategy and the specific role these indicators play:

- **The ADX used as a filter**

    - The ADX (average directional index) is used as a filter in this strategy and used to filter out unfavorable market conditions.

    - This strategy works best in sideways market conditions, when the ADX is below 25 the market is most likely moving in a sideways direction.

    - Therefore trades will only be taken when the ADX is below 25 (indicating a sideways market).

- **The VWAP used as the mean**

- This scalping strategy is a mean reversion strategy and based on the idea that when price deviates too far away from a mean (average) it is likely to revert back.

- The VWAP is a good indicator for using as a mean and often acts as a magnet, attracting the price back towards it.

- The VWAP is similar to a moving average, but it incorporates both price and volume. This makes it a more reliable mean than a simple moving average.

- **RSI is used for Precise Entry and Exit Points**

  - The RSI is used for pinpointing entries and exits in this strategy.

  - The length of the RSI is changed to 4 to be more responsive and detect changes in momentum sooner. The RSI will enter into the overbought and oversold zones before the actual price movement occurs.

Well-Defined Risk Management

This strategy includes a predefined stop loss of 5% and a take profit of 15% (1:3 risk/reward ratio). This risk/reward ratio is exceptionally profitable on any strategy with a 50% or higher win rate.

If you want to use this strategy for yourself on TradingView I have attached the pinescript code on the next page, you just have to copy it into TradingViews pine editor.

The Pine script code for this strategy:

/@version=4

```
strategy("VWAP, RSI, and ADX Mean Reversion Strategy", overlay=true)

// Inputs

vwap_length = input(20, "VWAP Length", minval=1)

rsi_length = input(4, "RSI Length", minval=1)

rsi_overbought = input(70, "RSI Overbought Level", minval=1)

rsi_oversold = input(30, "RSI Oversold Level", minval=1)

adx_length = input(14, "ADX Length", minval=1)

adx_level = input(25, "ADX Level", minval=1)

// Calculate VWAP and RSI

vwap = vwap(hlc3)

rsi = rsi(close, rsi_length)

// Calculate ADX

up = change(high)

down = -change(low)

trur = rma(tr, adx_length)

plus = fixnan(100 * rma(up > down and up > 0 ? up : 0, adx_length) / trur)

minus = fixnan(100 * rma(down > up and down > 0 ? down : 0, adx_length) / trur)

sum = plus + minus

adx = 100 * rma(abs(plus - minus) / (sum == 0 ? 1 : sum), adx_length)

// Plot VWAP and RSI

plot(vwap, "VWAP", color=color.blue)

plot(rsi, "RSI", color=color.purple)

// Entry and exit conditions

longCondition = close < vwap and rsi > rsi_overbought and adx < adx_level

if longCondition

    strategy.entry("Long", strategy.long)
```

```
shortCondition = close > vwap and rsi < rsi_oversold and adx < adx_level

if shortCondition

    strategy.entry("Short", strategy.short)

// Stop loss and take profit

stopLoss = input(2.0, "Stop Loss %", step=0.1) / 100

takeProfit = input(5.0, "Take Profit %", step=0.1) / 100

strategy.exit("Exit Long", "Long", stop=strategy.position_avg_price * (1 - stopLoss),
limit=strategy.position_avg_price * (1 + takeProfit))

strategy.exit("Exit Short", "Short", stop=strategy.position_avg_price * (1 + stopLoss),
limit=strategy.position_avg_price * (1 - takeProfit))
```

Analyzing Market Conditions

Understanding the current market environment is crucial because it helps you select the most suitable scalping strategy and adapt your approach accordingly.

Market conditions can generally be categorized into two main types:

Trending Markets:

In a trending market, the price moves steadily in a specific direction, either upwards (bullish) or downwards (bearish). This type of market offers excellent opportunities for momentum-based and trend-following scalping strategies.

To identify a trending market:

- Look for higher highs and higher lows in an uptrend or lower highs and lower lows in a downtrend.

- Use trend following indicators like moving averages to identify trend direction

- Use trend strength indicators like the ADX (Average Directional Index) or MACD to confirm the trend's strength.

Ranging Markets:

A ranging market, also known as a sideways market, is characterized by price fluctuations within a defined range, with no clear direction. In this type of market, mean reversion strategies work best, as they capitalize on price deviations from a central value, anticipating a return to the mean.

To identify a ranging market:

- Look for horizontal support and resistance levels and oscillating price movements between them.

- Look at moving average slopes, if moving average slopes appear flat the market is probably in a sideways range.

- Use the ADX indicator, if it is below 25 the market is most likely ranging.

Identifying the Primary and Secondary Trends

One of the key aspects of successful scalping lies in your ability to identify primary and secondary trends. Let's take a look at what exactly the "primary" and "secondary" trends are in trading, and why they are important for scalping.

Primary Trends – Trade in the direction of the primary/overall trend

Primary trends represent the overall market direction and can last for several months or even years. These long-term trends are the backbone of your scalping strategy, as they dictate the most profitable direction for your trades.

Aligning your trades with the primary trend increases your odds of success and enhances your overall trading performance.

To identify primary trends, follow these steps:

1. Choose a Higher Timeframe: Analyze a higher timeframe chart, such as the daily or weekly chart, to gain a broader perspective on the market direction.

2. Use Trend Following Indicators: Implement trend following indicators, such as moving averages or momentum indicators, to help you visualize the primary trend.

3. Market Structure: Evaluate the market structure by examining the arrangement of price highs and lows. An uptrend is characterized by higher highs and higher lows, while a downtrend exhibits lower highs and lower lows.

Secondary Trends – Use the secondary/short term trend for pinpointing entries/exits

Secondary trends are shorter-term fluctuations that occur within primary trends. For scalping, the secondary trend is simply the current timeframe you are using for entering and exiting trades.

Since scalping typically involves quick trades, you should use a low timeframe, such as the 1-minute or 5-minute chart. Trend following indicators can also be used to identify the secondary trend and help you fine-tune your entries and exits, maximizing your gains while minimizing your risk.

To identify secondary trends, follow these steps:

1. Choose a Lower Timeframe: Examine a lower timeframe chart, such as the 1-minute or 5-minute chart, to focus on short-term market fluctuations.

2. Use Trend Following Indicators: Employ trend following indicators, like moving averages or the Average Directional Index (ADX), to help you recognize the secondary trend within the primary trend.

3. Momentum Indicators: Utilize momentum indicators, such as the Relative Strength Index (RSI) or the Stochastic

oscillator, to gauge the strength of the secondary trend and anticipate potential reversals or continuations.

Examples of Primary and Secondary Trend Identification

Let's consider two examples to illustrate how to identify primary and secondary trends using different timeframes:

Example 1:

- Primary Trend: On the daily chart, the 200-day moving average is sloping upwards, and the market structure shows higher highs and higher lows, indicating an uptrend.

- Secondary Trend: On the 5-minute chart, the 50-period moving average is also sloping upwards, and the RSI remains above 50, suggesting a short-term uptrend within the primary trend.

Example 2:

- Primary Trend: On the weekly chart, a descending 50 day moving average, and the market structure displays lower lows, indicating a downtrend.

- Secondary Trend: On the 1-minute chart, the 20-period moving average is sloping upwards, and the Stochastic oscillator is crossed up above the centerline, indicating a short-term uptrend within the primary trend.

When both the primary and secondary trends are moving in the same direction, it can be an excellent opportunity to enter a trade, as it increases the likelihood of a successful outcome.

However, when the secondary trend is moving counter to the primary trend, it can also provide valuable opportunities, particularly for traders looking to capitalize on short-term market fluctuations.

Identifying "Buy the Dip" Opportunities

Suppose the primary trend is up, as evidenced by an upward-sloping moving average on a higher timeframe chart (e.g. daily or weekly) and a market structure consisting of higher highs and higher lows.

Meanwhile, the secondary trend on a lower timeframe chart (e.g., 1-minute or 5-minute) is down, with a downward-sloping moving average and momentum indicators signaling oversold conditions.

In this scenario, you can use the counter-trend movement in the secondary trend as an opportunity to "buy the dip". As the secondary trend moves down and approaches a key support level or an oversold reading on a momentum indicator, you can look to enter a long position, anticipating that the primary trend's strength will eventually resume and push the price higher.

Follow these steps to "buy the dip":

1. Identify Key Support Levels: Analyze the lower timeframe chart to find key support levels where the price might bounce, such as horizontal support lines, trend lines, or Fibonacci retracement levels.

2. Monitor Momentum Indicators: Keep an eye on momentum indicators like the RSI or Stochastic oscillator to detect oversold conditions, which can signal a potential reversal of the secondary trend.

3. Confirm the Reversal: Look for confirmation signals that the secondary trend is reversing back in the direction of the primary trend, such as bullish candlestick patterns, a crossover of moving averages, or a shift in momentum indicators from oversold to rising levels.

4. Enter the Trade: Once the reversal is confirmed, enter a long position with a stop-loss order placed below the key support level or recent swing low.

5. Set Profit Targets: Establish profit targets based on previous resistance levels, Fibonacci extensions, or a predetermined risk-reward ratio.

Types of Scalping Strategies

In this section, we will discuss the three main types of scalping strategies that traders use in the financial markets: Mean Reversion, Momentum, and AI-Based strategies.

Each of these strategies has unique characteristics and methods for generating trading signals. Understanding these differences will help you choose the best approach for your trading style.

#1: Mean Reversion

Mean reversion strategies are based on the concept that prices tend to revert to their average or equilibrium level over time. Scalpers who employ this approach capitalize on short-term deviations from the mean, expecting the price to return to its average level.

How Mean Reversion Strategies Work:

- Look for short-term price extremes as potential trading opportunities; identify overbought and oversold conditions in the market.

- Mean reversion strategies work best in sideways/range bound market conditions. You can use a filter like the ADX indicator to trade in these market conditions.

- Use strict risk management due to the possibility of price continuation rather than mean reversion

Common Indicators Used in Mean Reversion Strategies:

- Bollinger Bands: A volatility indicator that measures price deviations from a moving average, identifying potential overbought and oversold levels

- Relative Strength Index (RSI): A momentum oscillator that measures the speed and change of price movements, with overbought and oversold conditions represented by specific threshold levels

- Stochastic Oscillator: A momentum indicator that compares a security's closing price to its price range over a certain period, also identifying overbought and oversold levels

- VWAP: The VWAP (volume weighted average price) appears as a line, similar to a moving average. Essentially, the VWAP is a measure of the average price at which a security has traded throughout the day, weighted by the volume of trades at each price level.

Types of Mean Reversion Scalping Strategies

1. **Standard Deviation Scalping on Channel/Band Indicators:**

   - Capitalize on price deviations from the historical mean using channel or band indicators, such as Bollinger Bands.

   - Entry signals occur when price touches or crosses the bottom or top band. If price crosses the bottom band a buy/long signal occurs, conversely if price crosses the top band a sell/short signal is generated.

   - Exit the trade when price touches the mean or moving average.

2. **Overbought/Oversold Scalping on Momentum Oscillators:** •

   - Take advantage of short-term price deviations from the mean using momentum oscillators, such as RSI or Stochastic Oscillator.

   - A valid overbought/oversold signal will occur when the momentum oscillator enters the overbought/oversold zone and then crosses out of it.

   - Exit trades once the oscillator reaches a neutral level or the price approaches the mean.

#2: Momentum Scalping Strategies

Momentum scalping strategies focus on capitalizing on short-term price movements in the direction of the prevailing trend. Scalpers using momentum strategies aim to profit from strong price movements by entering and exiting trades quickly.

How Momentum Strategies Work

- Identify the trend: Determine the direction of the market trend (upward or downward) using technical analysis tools.

- Find entry points: Look for short-term price movements in the direction of the trend, using momentum indicators to identify potential trade opportunities.

- Quick trade execution: Enter and exit trades swiftly to capture small price movements, while keeping trade duration to a minimum.

- Risk management: Employ strict risk management techniques, such as stop-loss orders, to limit potential losses in case of trend reversals or unexpected price movements.

Common Indicators Used in Momentum Strategies

- Moving Averages: A popular trend-following indicator that smooths out price data, creating a line that traders can use to identify the direction of the trend.

- MACD (Moving Average Convergence Divergence): A momentum oscillator that calculates the difference between two moving averages, helping traders identify potential trend reversals or continuation patterns.

- RSI (Relative Strength Index): A momentum oscillator that measures the speed and change of price movements, with overbought and oversold conditions represented by specific threshold levels.

- ADX (Average Directional Index): A trend strength indicator that measures the strength of the current trend, allowing traders to identify strong trends suitable for momentum scalping strategies.

Types of Momentum Scalping Strategies

1. Breakout Scalping:

    - Capitalize on price breakouts from consolidation areas or key support and resistance levels.

    - Trade in the direction of the breakout, entering and exiting trades quickly to capture price movements.

2. Pullback Scalping:

    - Take advantage of short-term price retracements within the prevailing trend.

    - Identify potential entry points using support and resistance levels, moving averages, or Fibonacci retracement levels.

    - Execute trades in the direction of the trend, aiming to profit from the continuation of the trend after the retracement.

3. Divergence Scalping:

    - Leverage divergence on momentum indicators to predict potential market tops and bottoms, providing opportunities for short-term trades.

    - Identify divergences between price movements and momentum indicators, which could signal a potential reversal in the market.

    - Execute trades based on the divergence signals, aiming to profit from the anticipated market reversal. To ensure the divergence is valid, confirm it with a signal from a separate indicator or price breaking a support/resistance level.

Using Divergence in Momentum Scalping Strategies

Divergence occurs when the price action on a chart does not correspond with the movement of a momentum indicator. This discrepancy can signal a potential reversal in the market, providing opportunities for momentum scalpers to profit from short-term price movements. There are two types of divergence:

- **Regular Divergence**: Suggests a possible trend reversal.

  - Bullish Divergence: Occurs when the price forms lower lows while the momentum indicator forms higher lows. This suggests that the downtrend may be losing momentum, and a potential bullish reversal could follow.

  - Bearish Divergence: Occurs when the price forms higher highs while the momentum indicator forms lower highs. This indicates that the uptrend may be weakening, and a potential bearish reversal could ensue.

- **Hidden Divergence**: Suggests a trend continuation.

  - Bullish Hidden Divergence: Occurs when the price forms higher lows while the momentum indicator forms lower lows. This signals that the uptrend may continue, despite the temporary retracement.

  - Bearish Hidden Divergence: Occurs when the price forms lower highs while the momentum indicator forms higher highs. This suggests that the downtrend may persist, despite the brief retracement.

#3: AI/Machine Learning-Based Scalping Strategies

AI-Based scalping strategies employ machine learning algorithms and artificial intelligence to analyze market data and generate trading signals.

These strategies can adapt to changing market conditions and learn from historical data to improve their performance over time. In this section, we will explore the characteristics, types of algorithms, and examples of AI-Based scalping strategies.

Characteristics of AI-Based Strategies:

- Utilize advanced machine learning algorithms, such as neural networks, k-Nearest Neighbors, or Support Vector Machines

- Require computational resources and expertise in machine learning and programming

- Offer the potential for unique and innovative trading strategies that can adapt to market changes

- Can be combined with traditional technical indicators for enhanced decision-making

Common Machine Learning Algorithms Used in AI-Based Strategies:

- **Neural Networks:** A class of algorithms that mimics the structure and function of the human brain, used for pattern recognition and decision-making

- **k-Nearest Neighbors (kNN):** A non-parametric method used for classification and regression, which identifies the k closest data points to a new observation and makes predictions based on the majority class or average value

- **Support Vector Machines (SVM):** A type of supervised learning model that can be used for classification or regression, which constructs a hyperplane to separate classes or predict continuous values

Examples of AI-Based Scalping Strategies:
Neural Network-Based Scalping Strategy:

- Collect and preprocess historical market data for input into the neural network

- Train the neural network to identify patterns and relationships in the data that lead to profitable trades

- Implement the trained neural network in a trading system that generates and executes signals based on the AI's predictions

k-Nearest Neighbors (kNN) Scalping Strategy:

- Collect and preprocess historical market data for input into the kNN algorithm

- Train the kNN algorithm to identify the k closest data points to new observations and make predictions based on the majority class or average value

- Implement the trained kNN algorithm in a trading system that generates and executes signals based on the AI's predictions

Support Vector Machine (SVM) Scalping Strategy:

- Collect and preprocess historical market data for input into the SVM algorithm

- Train the SVM algorithm to construct a hyperplane that separates classes or predicts continuous values

- Implement the trained SVM algorithm in a trading system that generates and executes signals based on the AI's predictions

Chapter 2: Using Indicators in Scalping

When it comes to scalping, speed and precision are of the essence. Technical indicators, mathematical calculations derived from price, volume, or open interest, provide traders with valuable insights into the market's underlying forces.

Some key benefits of using indicators in scalping include:

- Speed and precision: In scalping, every second counts. Indicators help traders quickly identify and capitalize on short-term market movements, enabling split-second decisions with increased accuracy.

- Objective insights: Indicators provide data-driven analysis that eliminates the subjective biases that can cloud our judgment. This objectivity is crucial for scalpers seeking consistent results.

- Adaptability: As market conditions change, so do the effectiveness of certain indicators. By using a diverse array of indicators, scalpers can adjust their strategies on the fly, maximizing profits and minimizing risks.

Roles of Indicators in Scalping Strategies

1. Trend Confirmation: Indicators can be used to confirm the direction of the market, ensuring that scalpers only trade in the direction of the primary trend.

    - *Example*: Moving Averages can be employed to confirm an uptrend or downtrend, providing a clear signal to enter or exit a trade.

2. Filtering Signals: Indicators can help scalpers filter out false or low-quality signals, improving the overall effectiveness of their trading strategies.

    - *Example*: The ADX (Average Directional Index) can be used to gauge the strength of a trend, helping scalpers avoid trading during periods of low volatility or choppy market conditions.

3. Entry and Exit Points: Indicators can provide clear and precise entry and exit signals, enabling scalpers to optimize their trades for maximum profits.

- *Example*: The RSI (Relative Strength Index) can be utilized to identify overbought or oversold conditions, pinpointing the ideal moments to enter or exit a trade.

Implementing Indicators in Scalping Strategies

To incorporate indicators into a scalping strategy, follow these steps:

1. Select the indicators: Choose indicators that best aligns with what type of trading strategy you are using and market conditions you will be trading.

2. Optimize the settings: Fine-tune the parameters of your chosen indicators to maximize their effectiveness in the current market environment.

3. Combine indicators: Integrate multiple indicators to create a comprehensive, well-rounded strategy that capitalizes on the strengths of each.

4. Backtest and forward-test: Test your strategy using historical data and real-time market conditions to assess its performance and make necessary adjustments.

5. Execute: Put your strategy into action, and remember to monitor and adapt it as market conditions evolve.

In the following sections, we will explore various indicators and their applications in scalping strategies, allowing you to gain a deeper understanding of how they can be used to maximize profits and minimize risk.

Using Confirmation Indicators

Confirmation indicators are technical tools used by traders to provide additional evidence for a potential trade setup. These indicators help to confirm the validity of an entry or exit signal, increasing the probability of a successful trade. In the fast-paced world of scalping, having a clear and accurate signal is crucial. Confirmation indicators work in tandem with other indicators to strengthen the overall signal, enabling traders to make more informed decisions.

- Confirmation indicators add an extra layer of confidence to your trading signals.

- They increase the probability of a successful trade by validating the primary signal.

- In scalping, confirmation indicators are crucial for reducing false signals and improving overall trade accuracy.

The Value of Confirmation Indicators in Scalping

Scalping is a high-frequency trading strategy that requires precise entries and exits to capitalize on small price movements. Because of the short time frames involved, false signals can be detrimental to a scalper's overall success. Confirmation indicators play a vital role in minimizing false signals by adding an extra layer of validation to the primary trading signal.

- Confirmation indicators help reduce the number of false signals, which can be detrimental in scalping.

- They assist in making more accurate and confident trading decisions.

- In the fast-paced world of scalping, confirmation indicators are essential for maintaining a high win rate.

Confirmation Indicators vs. Filter Indicators

While both confirmation indicators and filter indicators are designed to improve the accuracy of trading signals, they serve different purposes. Confirmation indicators work by strengthening the primary signal, providing additional evidence that supports the trade. On the other hand, filter indicators work by eliminating potential false signals, reducing the number of overall trade signals.

- Confirmation indicators provide additional evidence to support the primary signal, increasing the likelihood of a successful trade.

- Filter indicators work by eliminating potential false signals, reducing the number of overall trade signals.

- Both types of indicators are essential for successful scalping, but they serve different purposes in the decision-making process.

How to Choose a Confirmation Indicator for your Strategy

When identifying potential confirmation indicators, it's essential to consider the characteristics of the primary indicator and how the confirmation indicator can complement it. Some factors to consider when selecting a confirmation indicator include:

1. **Type of primary indicator**: Consider whether your primary indicator is a trend-following or oscillating indicator. For example, if your primary indicator is a trend-following tool like a moving average, you might want to choose a confirmation indicator that measures the strength or momentum of the trend, such as the Relative Strength Index (RSI) or the Average Directional Index (ADX).

2. **Compatibility with the primary indicator**: Make sure the confirmation indicator is compatible with the primary indicator in terms of the time frame and the type of signals it generates. The confirmation indicator should provide additional evidence to support the primary signal without causing conflicting signals.

3. **Simplicity and ease of interpretation**: Choose confirmation indicators that are easy to understand and

interpret. Avoid overly complex indicators that may lead to confusion or misinterpretation of signals.

4. **Proven effectiveness**: Research the effectiveness of potential confirmation indicators in various market conditions and time frames. Look for indicators with a proven track record of success in complementing primary indicators and improving the accuracy of trading signals.

Examples of Good Primary and Confirmation Indicator Combinations

Here are some examples of primary and confirmation indicator combinations that can be effective in scalping strategies:

Example 1: MACD and RSI Combination

Primary Indicator: Relative Strength Index (RSI)

Confirmation Indicator: Moving Average Convergence Divergence (MACD)

How it works:

- The MACD is a trend-following momentum indicator.

- The RSI can be used to identify entries/exits using overbought/oversold conditions.

- When the MACD is crossed up, it can confirm the oversold (buy) signals from the RSI.

- When the MACD is crossed down, it can confirm the overbought (short) signals from the RSI.

Example 2: Bollinger Bands and Stochastic Oscillator Combination

Primary Indicator: Bollinger Bands

Confirmation Indicator: Stochastic Oscillator

How it works:

- Bollinger Bands are a volatility indicator that measures price movements relative to a moving average.

- The Stochastic Oscillator measures momentum and can confirm overbought or oversold conditions.

- When both indicators are in the overbought/oversold zones, a signal can be confirmed when the two stochastics lines crossover.

Example 3: Stochastic RSI & Supertrend

Primary Indicator: Stochastic RSI

Confirmation Indicator: Supertrend

How it works:

- The Stochastic RSI is an oscillator derived from the RSI, which measures the speed and change of price movements. It helps identify overbought or oversold conditions in the market.

- The Supertrend is a trend-following indicator that calculates average true range (ATR) to provide buy and sell signals. It helps to confirm the direction of the trend.

- The Supertrend can be used as a confirmation indicator to validate signals from the Stochastic RSI, helping traders to enter trades in the direction of the trend and avoid false signals.

Example 4: Parabolic SAR & On-Balance Volume (OBV)

Primary Indicator: Parabolic SAR

Confirmation Indicator: On-Balance Volume (OBV)

How it works:

- The Parabolic SAR is a trend-following indicator that generates buy and sell signals by calculating price and time. It provides entry and exit points as well as trailing stop-loss levels.

- The On-Balance Volume (OBV) is a momentum indicator that measures buying and selling pressure by analyzing cumulative trading volume.

- The OBV can be used as a confirmation indicator to ensure that there is sufficient buying or selling pressure to support the trade signals generated by the Parabolic SAR, thereby increasing the probability of a successful trade.

Using Leading and Lagging Indicators in Scalping

Use Leading Indicators as your Primary Indicator

Typically, the primary indicator in a trading strategy is a leading indicator, which helps traders anticipate future price movements. Leading indicators are often momentum oscillators that generate signals before significant price movements occur.

- **Momentum Oscillators**: These indicators measure the speed and change of price movements, providing early signals for potential trend reversals or continuations.

- **Examples**: Stochastic Oscillator, Relative Strength Index (RSI), Commodity Channel Index (CCI)

- **Role in Strategy**: Primary indicators help traders identify potential trade opportunities by providing early signals for price movements.

Use Lagging Indicators as your Confirmation Indicator

In many cases, the confirmation indicator is a lagging indicator, which helps traders confirm the primary signal by providing additional evidence based on historical price movements. Lagging indicators tend to be more reliable but generate signals after the price has already moved.

- **Trend-following Indicators**: These indicators follow price movements and provide confirmation of the trend's direction or strength.

- **Examples**: Moving Averages, Parabolic SAR, Supertrend

- **Role in Strategy**: Confirmation indicators help traders validate primary signals, reducing the risk of entering trades based on false signals.

Combining Two Leading Indicators in a Strategy

While it is common to use a leading indicator as the primary signal and a lagging indicator as the confirmation signal, it is also possible to use two leading indicators in combination, as demonstrated by the Bollinger Bands and Stochastic Oscillator example.

- **Purpose**: Combining two leading indicators can help traders capitalize on quick market movements and improve the overall responsiveness of the strategy.

- **Considerations**: When using two leading indicators, it's crucial to ensure that they complement each other and do not generate conflicting signals.

- **Example**: Bollinger Bands (volatility indicator) and Stochastic Oscillator (momentum oscillator) can be combined to identify overbought or oversold conditions while considering the market's volatility.

Using Filters in Scalping

Filters vs. Confirmation Indicators: What's the Difference?

While confirmation indicators help validate the primary signal by providing evidence of the trend's direction or strength, filter indicators serve a different purpose. Filter indicators are designed to identify specific market conditions, such as sideways or trending markets, and help traders filter out false signals generated by the primary indicator.

- **Filter Indicators**: These indicators focus on determining the prevailing market condition rather than the direction of the trend.

- **Purpose:** Filter indicators help traders avoid entering trades based on false signals generated by primary indicators during unfavorable market conditions.

Why Filters are Important

Using a filter indicator to identify market conditions is crucial for several reasons:

- **Indicator Performance:** Certain indicators perform better in specific market conditions. For example, trend-following indicators may generate false signals during sideways markets, while oscillators can produce misleading signals in strong trending markets.

- **Improved Accuracy:** By filtering out signals that occur during unfavorable market conditions, traders can improve the accuracy of their trading strategy and increase the probability of successful trades.

- **Risk Management:** By avoiding trades during unfavorable conditions, traders can minimize their exposure to unnecessary risks and preserve their trading capital.

Understanding How Market Conditions Affect Indicators

Different market conditions can significantly impact the performance of various indicators:

- **Sideways Market Conditions**: In a sideways or range-bound market, trend-following indicators, such as moving averages or the MACD, can produce false signals as the price oscillates within a narrow range. Oscillators like the RSI or Stochastic Oscillator tend to perform better in these conditions, as they can identify overbought or oversold levels within the range.

- **Trending Market Conditions:** During strong trending markets, trend-following indicators, such as moving averages, Parabolic SAR, or the ADX, can provide more accurate signals. Oscillators, on the other hand, may stay in overbought or oversold territory for extended periods, leading to false reversal signals.

By incorporating filter indicators into their trading strategy, traders can ensure that they only enter trades when the market conditions are favorable for their chosen primary indicator, improving the overall performance and accuracy of their strategy.

Let's take a look at some effective filter indicators you can use in your scalping strategy.

Indicator Filters for Scalping

Here are some of the best indicator filters you can use for scalping, these indicators will help you identify and filter for the best market conditions for your strategy.

Filter #1: The ADX

The ADX is a trend strength indicator that can help you identify trending or sideways markets. It ranges from 0 to 100, with higher values indicating a stronger trend.

- A commonly used threshold is 25. If the ADX is above 25, it suggests a trending market, while an ADX below 25 indicates a sideways or weakly trending market.

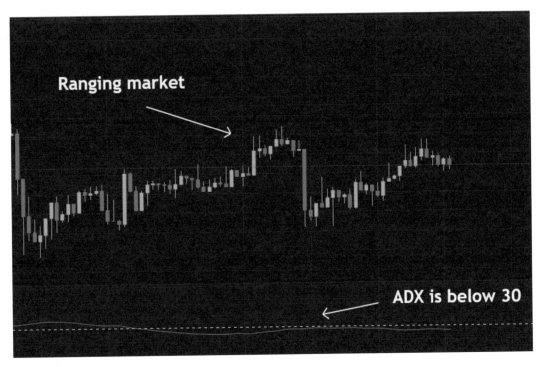

Example of the ADX below 30 indicating a ranging market

Filter #2: Breakout/Consolidation Filter

The Breakout/Consolidation Filter is one of my favorite indicators for identifying ranging/trending markets. This is a free indicator found on TradingView that was created by the TradingView community.

To Find this Indicator:

- Open the indicator search box on TradingView

- Type **Breakout/Consolidation Filter [jwammo12]** in the indicator search box

The author of this indicator is jwammo12 as seen in the screenshot above.

How it Works

This indicator is similar to the ADX, using a single line that moves up or down based on how strong the current trend is.

- If this indicator is below 50, price is in a period of consolidation

- If this indicator is above 50, price is trending and not consolidating

This indicator includes a yellow line at the 50 level to make it easier to see these signals.

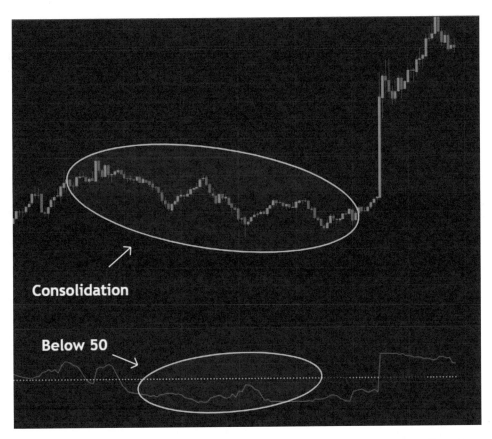

Example of the Breakout/Consolidation Filter under 50 indicating price is ranging

As you can see in the screenshot above, this indicator works very well for identifying ranges, breakouts of consolidation and trends.

For mean reversion trading:

- Only enter trades if the Breakout/Consolidation Filter is **under 50.**

For trend trading:

- Only enter trades if the Breakout/Consolidation Filter is **above 50.**

Filter #3: Moving Averages

Moving averages are among the most commonly used filters to identify market trends. They smooth out price data, making it easier to spot a trend.

You can use a single moving average or a combination of two moving averages with different timeframes.

- **Single Moving Average**: Choose a suitable period for the moving average (e.g., 50, 100, or 200). If the price stays consistently above the moving average, it suggests an uptrend, while if it stays below the moving average, it indicates a downtrend. If the price oscillates around the moving average, it implies a sideways market.

- **Dual Moving Averages**: Use two moving averages with different periods (e.g., 20 and 50). When the shorter-period moving average (20) crosses above the longer-period moving average (50), it signals the beginning of an uptrend. Conversely, when the shorter-period moving average crosses below the longer-period moving average, it suggests a downtrend. If the moving averages frequently intersect, it indicates a sideways market.

Below is an example of using two moving averages to identify a sideways trending market. Note how the long term MA appears flat, and the short term MA is frequently crossing above/below the long term MA.

Example of dual moving averages indicating a sideways market

Choosing Your Primary Indicator

In this section, we will discuss primary indicators, their significance in a scalping strategy, and how to select the right primary indicator for your trading setup. Remember, primary indicators should be "leading" indicators that produce accurate signals for optimal results.

What Makes a Good Primary Indicator for Scalping?

When choosing a primary indicator for your scalping strategy, consider the following:

1. **Leading Indicators**: Primary indicators should ideally be leading indicators that produce signals ahead of price movements.

    - This is essential for scalping, as it allows traders to capitalize on short-term price fluctuations quickly.

2. **Accurate Signals**: Primary indicators must generate accurate signals, minimizing false or misleading entry and exit points.

   - This helps traders maintain a high win rate and minimizes losses.

3. **Ease of Interpretation**: The primary indicator should be simple enough for traders to understand and interpret its signals.

   - This allows for quick decision-making in the fast-paced environment of scalping.

Examples of Good Primary Indicators for Scalping

Here are some popular primary indicators used in scalping strategies:

- **Bollinger Bands**

  Signals generated when the price touches or crosses the upper or lower bands, indicating overbought or oversold conditions.

  These signals can be accurate in identifying potential reversals in sideways market conditions.

- **Relative Strength Index (RSI)**

  Signals generated when the RSI crosses overbought or oversold levels, these signals indicate potential trend reversals and price exhaustion

  RSI divergence signals can be used in trending markets to identify trend reversals.

- **Stochastic Oscillator**

  Signals generated by crossovers between the %K and %D lines, this indicates momentum shifts and potential trend reversals. These crossover signals work best in sideways market conditions.

Divergence can also be used on the SO to identify trend reversals in trending market conditions.

- **KDJ**

  A variation of the Stochastic Oscillator, consisting of three lines: %K, %D, and %J

  Provides additional smoothing and sensitivity adjustments compared to the traditional Stochastic Oscillator

  Signals generated by crossovers between the %K, %D, and %J lines, as well as overbought and oversold conditions.

Steps for Selecting a Primary Indicator

1. **Define Your Trading Objective**: Determine the primary goal of your advanced scalping strategy (e.g., capturing small price movements with increased precision, exploiting specific market inefficiencies, or employing advanced mean reversion techniques).

2. **Identify Market Conditions for Trading**: Assess the market conditions you plan to trade in, such as trending or range-bound markets, and consider the indicators that perform best in those conditions.

3. **Analyze Indicator Correlations**: Analyze the correlations between different primary indicators to ensure that they provide unique and complementary information, reducing the risk of over-reliance on a single indicator.

4. **Test the Indicator**: Backtest and forward test the indicator to ensure it produces accurate signals and meets your desired win rate, even in changing market conditions.

5. **Optimize the Indicator**: Fine-tune the indicator settings to optimize its performance for your advanced scalping strategy, taking into account the specific market conditions you plan to trade in.

6. **Implement the Indicator**: Incorporate the primary indicator into your trading strategy, and continually monitor its performance and effectiveness.

Selecting a primary indicator for entries and exits is crucial in developing a successful scalping strategy.

By understanding the characteristics of primary indicators, evaluating their performance, and optimizing their settings, you can maximize the profitability of your scalping strategy.

Chapter 3: Advanced Indicator Signals for Scalping

In this chapter, we will delve into advanced indicator entry and exit signals for scalping. As a scalper, it is essential to have a thorough understanding of these signals to identify profitable opportunities and optimize your trading strategy.

With the proper application of advanced indicators, you can improve your win rate and potentially increase your overall profitability.

In this chapter we will cover:

- **Scalping Indicator Entry/Exit Signals:** Discover a selection of advanced scalping indicators that can provide high-probability entry and exit signals. Learn how to utilize these indicators effectively to enhance your trading strategy.

  - Scalp Pro

  - Quantitative Qualitative Estimation (QQE)

  - Harmonic Patterns Based Trend Follower

  - Supertrend ANY INDICATOR

  - And more

- **Machine Learning and Algorithmic Indicator Scalping Signals:** Explore the power of artificial intelligence and machine learning in generating scalping signals. Gain insights into cutting-edge strategies that leverage these technologies to make informed trading decisions.

  - Machine Learning: kNN-based Strategy

  - Machine Learning: Lorentzian Classification

- Auto Harmonic Patterns - V2

Throughout this chapter, we will provide detailed explanations and practical examples of how to implement these advanced indicator entry and exit signals into your scalping strategy.

How to Find These Indicators

This chapter includes highly accurate buy/sell signals from indicators found on the charting platform TradingView. These are free indicators that other traders have created and published on TradingView.

- Make a TradingView account (TradingView.com), you can sign up for a free account if you don't want to pay.

- Open up a chart on TradingView, and click on the "indicators" icon found at the top toolbar, then search the indicator you are looking for.

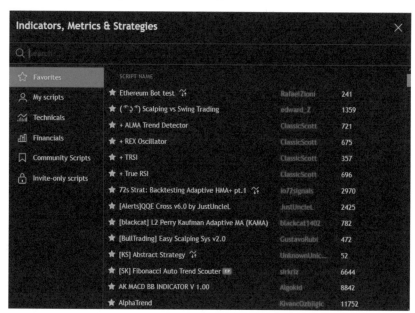

The TradingView indicator search box

Scalping Indicator Signal #1: False Breakout (Expo)

By: Zeiierman

To find this indicator type "False Breakout (Expo)" in the indicator search box

Overview:

"False Breakout (Expo)" designed to identify and visualize false breakouts in the market. False breakouts occur when the price moves beyond a support or resistance level but quickly reverses, trapping traders who entered positions based on the initial breakout. When a false breakout occurs this is typically a sign of a trend reversal.

This indicator works best in sideway/range bound market conditions.

Indicator Tip:

- For better scalping signals enable "aggressive" in the indicator settings

Buy Signal:

- A false break of support occurs and a green triangle appears below price

Sell Signal:

- A false break of support occurs and a red triangle appears above price

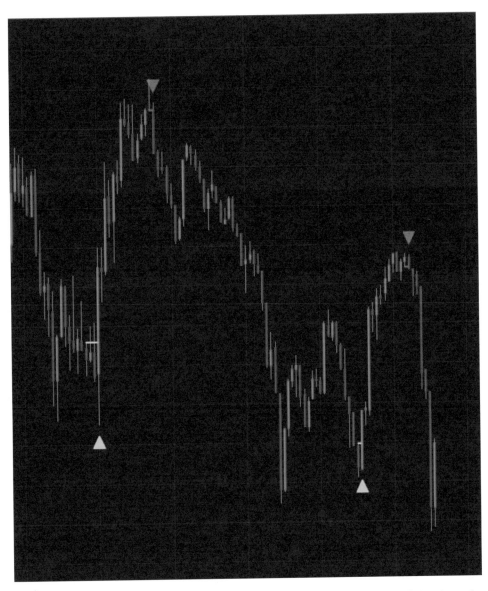

Example of buy (green triangle) and sell (red triangle) signals using this indicator

Scalping Indicator Signal #2: Scalp Pro

By ovelix

To find this indicator type "Scalp Pro" in the indicator search box

Overview:

The Scalp Pro is a momentum-based oscillator that uses a combination of moving averages and exponential smoothing (similar to the MACD) to generate buy and sell signals.

The indicator is plotted as two lines: the faster line (yellow) and the slower line (green). The crossing of these lines generates buy and sell signals. When the faster line crosses above the slower line, a buy signal is generated, and when the faster line crosses below the slower line, a sell signal is generated.

To reduce false signals with this indicator, use it in combination with a filter indicator.

Indicator Tip:

Use the following settings:

Fast Line = 10

Slow Line = 12

Smoothness = 12

Buy Signal:

The fast line crosses above the slow line and a "buy" label appears

Sell Signal:

The slow line crosses above the fast line and a "sell" label appears

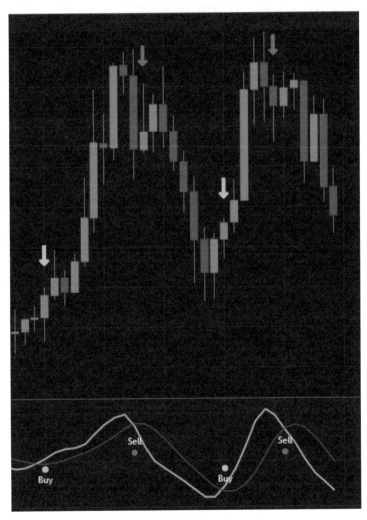

Example of buy and sell signals using the "Scalp Pro" indicator

Scalping Indicator Signal #3: Quantitative Qualitative Estimation QQE

By: KivancOzbilgic

To find this indicator type "Quantitative Qualitative Estimation QQE" in the indicator search box

Overview:

The QQE is primarily based on the Relative Strength Index (RSI) and uses a combination of moving averages and ATR values to generate trading signals. This indicator is designed to produce fewer false signals in sideways markets and accurately predict market tops and bottoms.

The QQE indicator generates trading signals based on the crossovers between a fast and slow line.

Indicator Tip:

Use the following settings:

- RSI Length = 14

- SF RSI Smoothing Factor = 10

Buy Signal:

- The fast line crosses above the slow and a "Buy" arrow appears on the QQE

Sell Signal:

- The slow line crosses above the fast and a "Sell" arrow appears on the QQE

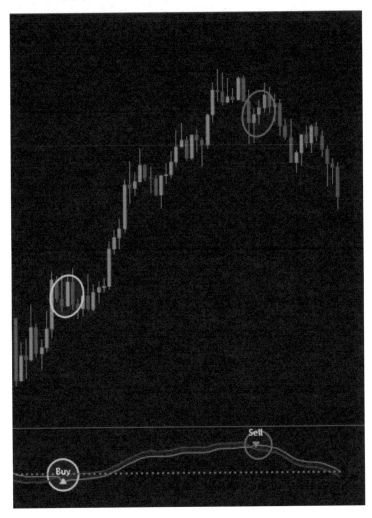

Example of buy and sell signals using the QQE indicator

Scalping Indicator Signal #4: On-chart Wavetrend Divergence with Pivots

By: AdonisWerther

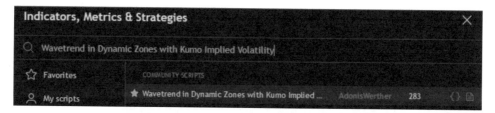

To find this indicator type "Wavetrend in Dynamic Zones with Kumo Implied Volatility" in the indicator search box

Overview:

The "On-chart Wavetrend Divergence with Pivots" indicator is an excellent choice for scalping strategies due to its combination of the Wavetrend oscillator, divergence detection, and pivot points.

The Wavetrend oscillator provides timely buy and sell signals by indicating momentum shifts, while the divergence detection helps identify potential market turning points by highlighting when the price and the indicator move in opposite directions.

Pivot points offer critical support and resistance levels, which scalpers can use to set entry and exit points, as well as stop-loss and take-profit orders.

By combining these features, this indicator helps scalpers identify high-probability trading opportunities based on momentum, trend exhaustion, and significant support and resistance levels.

Buy Signals:

- A green dot appears below price
- Price is at the S1 pivot

Sell Signals:

- A red dot appears above price
- Price is at the R1 pivot

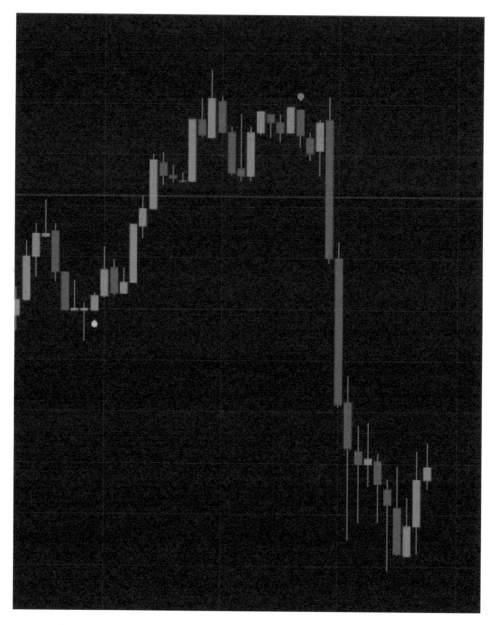

Example of buy (green dot) and sell (red dot) signals using this indicator

Scalping Indicator Signal #5: Harmonic Patterns Based Trend Follower

By: HeWhoMustNotBeNamed

To find this indicator type "Harmonic Patterns Based Trend Follower" in the indicator search box

Overview:

The indicator identifies harmonic patterns in the price data and uses them to predict potential price reversals. Harmonic patterns are geometric price structures based on Fibonacci ratios and are used to identify potential reversal points in the market.

The Harmonic Patterns Based Trend Follower also incorporates a trend-following element to filter the signals, ensuring that trades are only executed in the direction of the prevailing trend. This increases the probability of successful trades by avoiding counter-trend signals.

Indicator Tip:

Use the following settings for scalping

- Base = correction

- Entry % = 85

- Stop % = 5

Buy Signals:

- A bullish harmonic pattern is detected, suggesting a potential reversal from a downtrend to an uptrend.

- The trend-following element of the indicator confirms that the prevailing trend is bullish or that there is a bullish reversal in progress (candle color will change green).

- Once both conditions are met, the indicator generates a buy signal, indicating a potential long entry point.

Sell Signals:

- A bearish harmonic pattern is detected, suggesting a potential reversal from an uptrend to a downtrend.

- The trend-following element of the indicator confirms that the prevailing trend is bearish or that there is a bearish reversal in progress (candle color will change green).

- Once both conditions are met, the indicator generates a sell signal, indicating a potential short entry point.

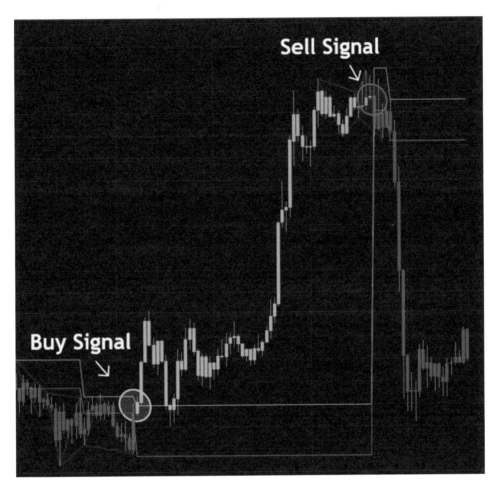

Example of buy (green circle) and sell (red circle) signals using the Harmonic Patterns Based Trend Follower indicator

Scalping Indicator Signal #6: Supertrend ANY INDICATOR

By: wbburgin

To find this indicator type "Supertrend ANY INDICATOR" in the indicator search box

Overview:

This versatile indicator combines the Supertrend indicator with a variety of other technical indicators, such as the RSI, MFI, or CCI, to generate buy and sell signals. Additionally, it incorporates a range filter to help filter out false signals during range-bound or sideways markets.

The supertrend indicator is a trend-following indicator that uses price and volatility to determine the direction of the trend. It consists of a moving average line and an upper and lower band that adjusts based on the asset's volatility.

When a signal occurs, the indicator color will change red or green depending on the signal, and a "Buy" or "Sell" will also appear on the indicator making it easy to identify signals.

Indicator Tip:

Change the following settings

- Indicator for Supertrend = RSI

- Enable "Use Range Filter of Indicator"

- Range Filter Multiple = 5

Buy Signals:

- The supertrend crosses up and the color changes green
- A "Buy" appears on the supertrend

Sell Signals:

- The supertrend crosses down and the color changes red
- A "Sell" appears on the supertrend

Scalping Indicator Signal #7: Fair Value Bands

By: quantifytools

To find this indicator, type "fair value bands" in the indicator search box on TradingView (by quantifytools)

Overview:

The fair value bands indicator is a indicator similar to the Bollinger Bands but is calculated using a proprietary algorithm that aims to provide more accurate entries and exits, with fewer false signals.

The Fair Value Bands consist of three bands, these include - 1x deviation, 2x deviation, 3x deviation bands.

All of these bands can be used for entry/exit signals, but the most accurate signals occur when price touches the 3x deviation band. The 3x deviation band appears as a zone rather than a single line.

The basis (middle) line will also change colors depending on the trend direction. The visual style of this indicator makes it easy identify entry/exit signals.

Buy Signals:

- Price touches or enters the zone of the bottom 3x deviation band

Sell Signals:

- Price touches or enters the zone of the bottom 3x deviation band

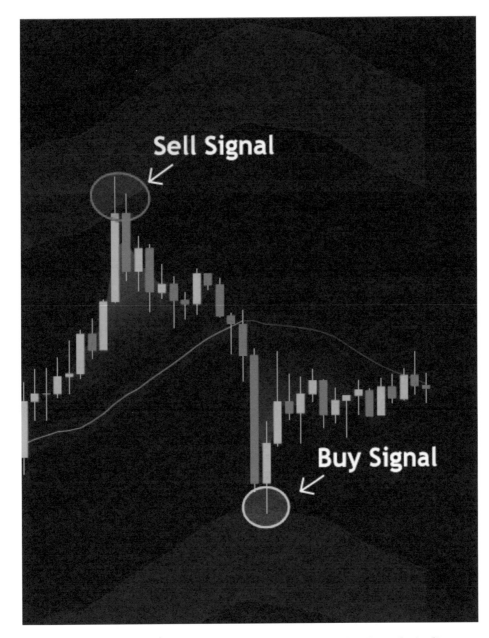

Example of a buy and sell signal on the fair value bands indicator

Scalping Indicator Signal #8: Leading MACD (Expo)

By: Zeiierman

To find this indicator, type "Leading MACD (Expo)" in the indicator search box on TradingView

Overview:

This is modified MACD indicator that is designed to be a leading indicator rather then the regular MACD which is a lagging indicator. You can use this MACD as a primary indicator for entries/exits. The signals that this indicator generates are surprisingly accurate and great for scalping.

Buy Signals:

- The fast MACD line crosses above the slow line

- The histogram color changes green

Sell Signals:

- The fast MACD line crosses below the slow line

- The histogram color changes red

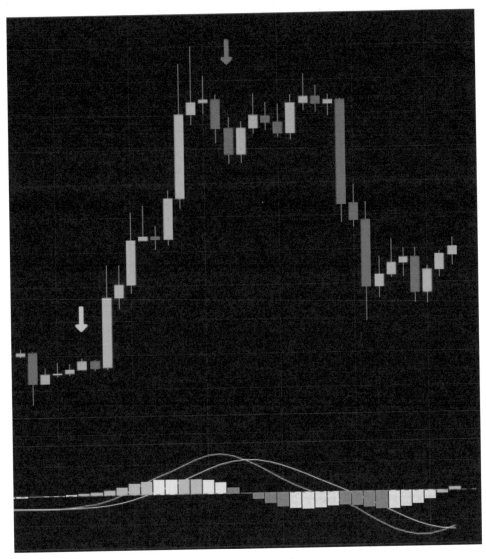

Example of buy and sell signals on the Leading MACD (Expo)

Scalping Indicator Signal #9: CM Pivot Bands V1

By: ChrisMoody

To find this indicator, type "CM Pivot Bands" in the indicator search box on TradingView (by ChrisMoody)

Overview:

The CM Pivot Bands indicator on TradingView is a powerful tool for identifying key levels of support and resistance in the market. It is based on the concept of pivot points and combines several different calculations to provide a comprehensive view of market conditions. The indicator displays bands around a central pivot line, with the upper and lower bands representing resistance and support levels.

The central pivot line is calculated using the previous day's high, low, and close prices, and can be used to identify key levels of support and resistance.

When price action moves into the upper or lower bands, it can indicate a potential reversal.

Indicator Tip:

- This indicator is the most effective in sideways market conditions

Buy Signals:

- Price touches the bottom (green) band

Sell Signals:

- Price touches the upper (red) band

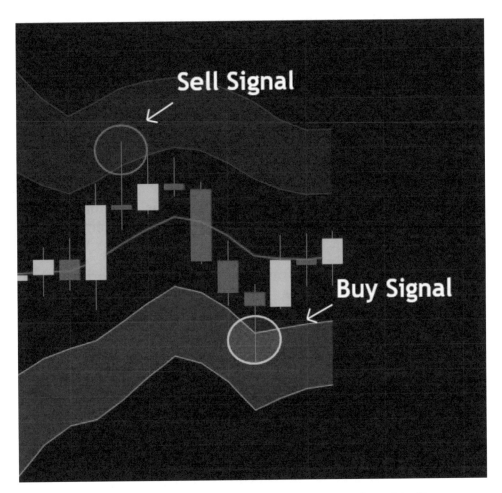

Example of a buy and sell signal on the CM pivot band indicator

Machine learning and Algorithmic Indicator Scalping Signals

These indicators harness the power of advanced algorithms and machine learning models to generate more accurate and adaptive trade signals, leading to higher win rates and more profitable trades.

How AI-Based Indicators Work:

1. **Data Collection and Preprocessing**

   - AI algorithms require large datasets to learn from and make predictions. Data can include historical price movements, technical indicators, and other relevant market factors.

   - Data preprocessing involves cleaning, normalization, and feature engineering, which are crucial steps in preparing the data for machine learning models.

2. **Model Selection and Training**

   - Traders can choose from various machine learning models, such as neural networks, reinforcement learning, and decision trees.

   - The model is trained on a subset of historical data to learn patterns and relationships between input features (e.g., indicators) and the target variable (e.g., future price movements).

3. **Model Validation and Optimization**

   - The trained model is tested on a separate dataset to evaluate its performance and accuracy.

   - Traders can fine-tune model parameters and features to improve performance, reduce overfitting, and adapt to changing market conditions.

Now let's take a look at some advanced algorithmic and AI based indicators you can use in your scalping strategies.

AI/Algorithmic Indicator Signal #1: Goethe A - Multiple Leading Indicator Package

By: AdonisWerther

To find this indicator type "Goethe A - Multiple Leading Indicator Package" in the indicator search box

Overview:

The Goethe A Indicator Package is a versatile and comprehensive tool that combines multiple leading and lagging indicators, making it a great choice for scalping strategies. It provides traders with insights into local trends, support and resistance levels, trend reversals, and potential entry and exit points through various components such as OBV/VPT divergences, smoothed Heikin-Ashi, daily pivots, and more.

Buy/sell signals will appear as different color triangles and circles on your chart depending the specific signal.

Indicator Tip:

- To make the buy/sell signals easier to see, turn off the "Pivot High" and "Pivot Low" signals in the settings

Buy Signal:

- Green circle or blue triangle appear below price

Sell Signal

- Red circle or orange triangle appear above price

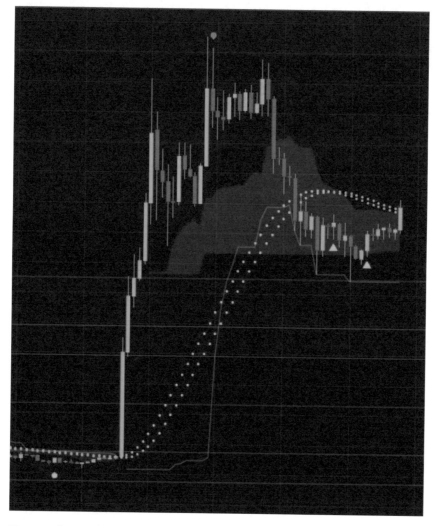

Example of buy and sell signals using the Goethe A - Multiple Leading Indicator Package

AI/Algorithmic Indicator Signal #2: Machine Learning: kNN-based Strategy

By: capissimo

To find this indicator type "Machine Learning: kNN-based Strategy" in the indicator search box

Overview:

The kNN-based strategy in this indicator is designed to predict the next candle's direction, i.e., whether the market will go up or down. It does so by analyzing historical price data and finding the most similar patterns to the current market situation. The strategy then assigns a label (up or down) based on the majority vote of the k nearest neighbors.

When a buy or sell signal is generated a blue or red label will appear above/below the candle.

Buy Signal:

- A blue label appears below a candle

Sell Signal:

- A red label appears above a candle

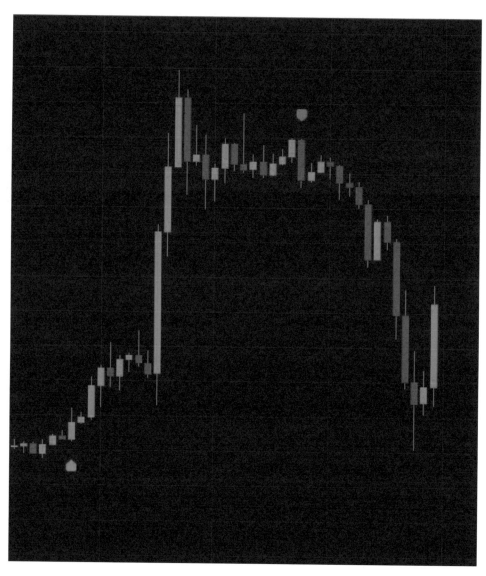

Buy (blue label) and sell (red label) signals using the Machine Learning: kNN-based Strategy indicator

AI/Algorithmic Indicator Signal #3: Machine Learning: Lorentzian Classification

By: jdehorty

To find this indicator type "Machine Learning: Lorentzian Classification" in the indicator search box

Overview:

This indicator uses a machine learning algorithm to analyze historical price data and make predictions about future price movements. The algorithm is based on the Lorentzian distribution, which can help capture and model complex patterns in the data.

These signals can be either bullish or bearish, indicating the predicted direction of the price movement.

Users can modify the indicator's settings to suit their trading style and preferences. They can adjust parameters such as the lookback period, the number of features used in the algorithm, and the classification threshold.

Indicator Tip:

- The user can add filters in the indicator settings, such as using the 200 EMA as a trend filter or an ADX filter, to further refine the signals generated by this indicator.

  By applying such filters, the user can reduce the number of false signals generated and increase the accuracy of the buy and sell signals.

Buy Signal:

- A green buy signal appears below a candle

- The moving average line color changes green

Sell Signal:

- A red sell signal appears above a candle

- The moving average line color changes red

AI/Algorithmic Indicator Signal #4: Auto Harmonic Patterns - V2

By: HeWhoMustNotBeNamed

To find this indicator type "Auto Harmonic Patterns - V2" in the indicator search box

Overview:

This indicator automatically detects harmonic patterns in price charts, helping traders identify potential trading opportunities based on these patterns. Harmonic patterns are a series of geometric price structures that follow specific Fibonacci ratios, which can help predict potential reversals in the market.

This indicator highlights potential reversal zones (PRZ) for each detected pattern. These zones are price levels where the harmonic pattern is expected to complete, and a reversal is likely to occur. Traders can use these zones as potential entry points or profit targets.

Indicator Tip:

Change the following settings

- Enable alternative source: close

Buy Signal:

- A buy signal is generated when a bullish harmonic pattern is detected, and the price reaches the potential reversal zone (PRZ) associated with the pattern.

- A price target (green line) will appear above price

Sell Signal:

- A sell signal is generated when a bearish harmonic pattern is detected, and the price reaches the potential reversal zone (PRZ) associated with the pattern.

- A price target (green line) will appear below price

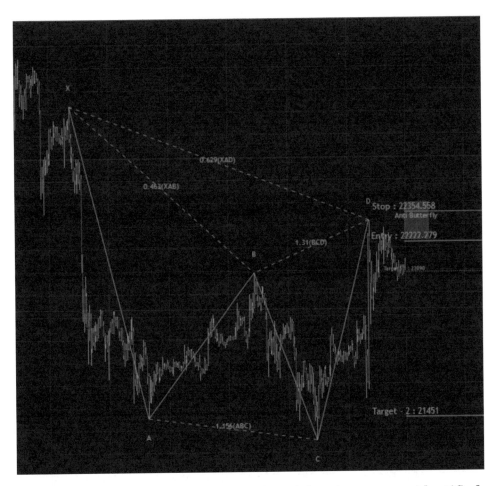

An example of a sell signal with a bearish price pattern identified, note the price target (green line) is below price

Chapter 4: High Win Rate Advanced Scalping Strategies

In this chapter, we will dive deep into some of the most effective and unique scalping strategies that can help you achieve impressive gains scalping the markets.

These strategies have been designed with practicality and ease of implementation in mind, so you can quickly incorporate them into your trading arsenal. We will provide step-by-step instructions to help you understand and execute each strategy effectively.

Each strategy will include the following sections:

- **Overview:** A brief explanation of the strategy, its rationale, and its core principles

- **Indicator Setup:** The necessary indicators and their settings for the strategy

- **Entry/Exit Conditions:** A detailed walkthrough of the strategy, including entry and exit signals, risk management, and trade management

Keep in mind that while these strategies are designed to achieve high win rates, no strategy is foolproof, and implementing effective risk management is crucial for long-term success. Before using these strategies you should backtest and papertrade them on a practice account first.

Scalping Strategy #1: False Breakout + MACD

Strategy Indicators:

- ADX

- Leading MACD (Expo)

- 500 EMA

- False Breakout (Expo)

  Use settings: False Breakout Period = 15, New Breakout = 3, Signal Valid = 3

  Enable the "Aggressive" box

Strategy Overview:

This strategy uses the False Breakout indicator to identify entries when a false breakout occurs. The leading MACD indicator is used to confirm the false breakout signals. This strategy works best in sideways market conditions and uses the ADX as a filter to only take trades in these market conditions.

The 500 EMA is used to trade in the direction of the overall trend.

Buy/Long Conditions:

- Price is above the 500 EMA

- The ADX is below 30

- The MACD is crossed up and the histogram is green

- Enter long when a buy signal (green triangle) occurs on the False Breakout indicator

- Place stop loss below the entry candle

- Exit long when the MACD crosses down and the histogram turns red

Sell/Short Conditions:

- Price is below the 500 EMA

- The ADX is below 30

- The MACD is crossed down and the histogram is red

- Enter short when a sell signal (red triangle) occurs on the False Breakout indicator

- Place stop loss above the entry candle

- Exit short when the MACD crosses up and the histogram turns green

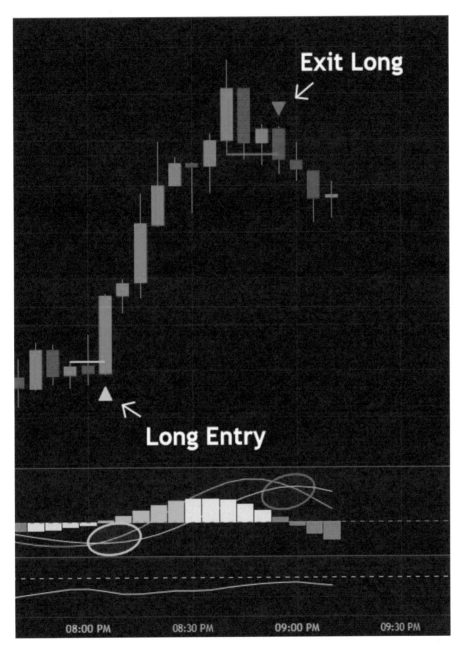

Example of a long entry and exit using this strategy

Scalping Strategy #2: Bollinger Band Reversal Strategy

Strategy Indicators:

- Bollinger band (default settings)

- 200 EMA

- Reversal finder indicator (by NS91)

- Breakout/Consolidation Filter (by jwammo12)

Strategy Overview:

This is a mean reversion trading strategy that is designed for scalping in rangebound/sideways market conditions. The breakout/consolidation filter is used to identify and take trades in these conditions.

The Bollinger bands and reversal finder are used for entries and exits.

Buy/Long Conditions:

- The breakout/consolidation filter is below 50

- Price is above the 200 EMA

- Price is outside or touching the bottom Bollinger band

- A green dot appears under the candle

- Exit long when price touches the top Bollinger band or a red dot appears

Sell/Short Conditions:

- The breakout/consolidation filter is below 50

- Price is below the 200 EMA

- Price is outside or touching the top Bollinger band

- Red dot appears above the candle

- Exit short when price touches the bottom Bollinger bands or a green dot appears

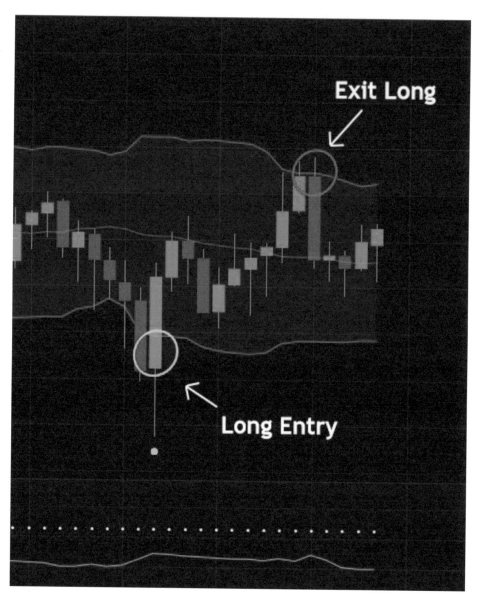

A long entry and exit using this scalping strategy

Scalping Strategy #3: Williams %R Scalping Strategy

Strategy Indicators:

- Williams %R (by Stuehmer on TradingView)

- ADX

- CM Pivot Bands V1 (by ChrisMoody on TradingView)

   *Change the length to 20

Strategy Overview:

This is a scalping strategy using the CM pivot bands indicator and the Williams %R (the willy) indicators for scalping short term price swings in the market.

When price touches the top or bottom of the CM pivot bands it will likely act as support/resistance levels where price will reverse.

The Williams %R indicator used in this strategy is similar to the RSI. This version of the Williams %R indicator uses a moving average for identifying signals.

This strategy will work the best in sideways/rangebound markets, the ADX is used to filter out trending market conditions.

Buy/Long Conditions:

- The ADX is below 25

- Candles are closing in the bottom green band

- Enter long when the Williams%R crosses above the MA

- Exit long when price touches the top red band or the Williams%R crosses below the MA

Sell/Short Conditions

- The ADX is below 25

- Candles are closing in the top red band

- Enter short when the Williams%R crosses below the MA

- Exit short when price touches the bottom green band or the Williams%R crosses above the MA

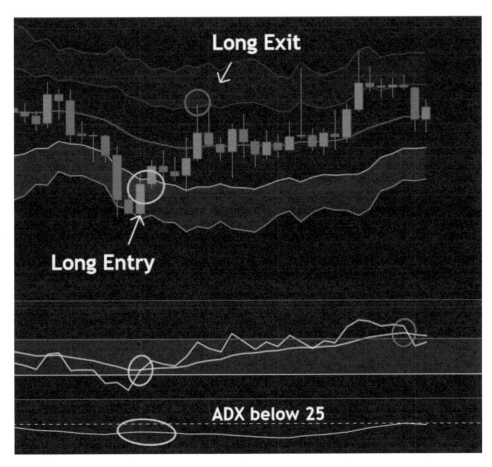

Example of a long entry and exit using this strategy

Scalping Strategy #4: Harmonic Patterns Based Trend Follower

Strategy Indicators:

- 500 EMA

- Quantitative Qualitative Estimation QQE

  Use these settings:

  - SF RSI Smoothing Factor = 20

- Harmonic Patterns Based Trend Follower

  Use these settings:

  - Base = correction

  - Entry % = 85

  - Stop % = 5

Strategy Overview:

This strategy uses a the Harmonic Patterns Based Trend Follower (HP-TF) for entries and the QQE as a confirmation indicator. The QQE and HP-TF are designed to avoid false signals in sideways market conditions, which makes a great combination for identifying trends and trend reversals, even in choppy markets.

The 500 EMA is used to identify and trade in the direction of the overall trend.

Buy/Long Conditions:

- Price is above the 500 EMA

- A buy signal appears on the QQE and it is crossed up

- Enter long when a buy signal occurs on the HP-TF (candle color changes green), place stoploss below the entry candle

- Exit long when a sell signal occurs on the QQE or HP-TF (candle color changes red)

Sell/Short Conditions:

- Price is below the 500 EMA

- A sell signal appears on the QQE and it is crossed down

- Enter short when a sell signal occurs on the HP-TF (candle color changes red), place stoploss above the entry candle

- Exit short when a buy signal occurs on the QQE or HP-TF (candle color changes green)

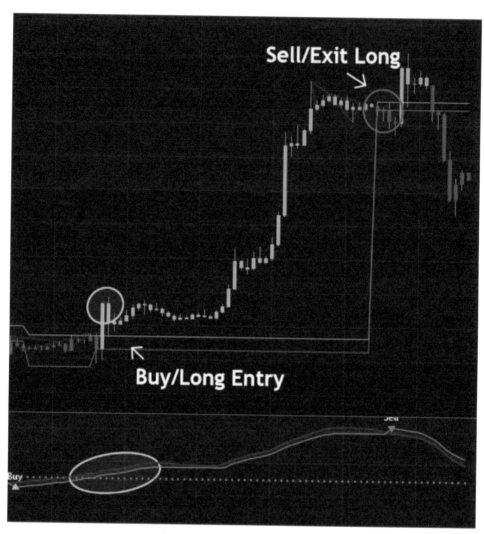

Example of a long entry using this strategy

Scalping Strategy #5: Machine Learning kNN Strategy

Strategy Indicators:

- Machine Learning: kNN-based Strategy

- 500 EMA

- ADX (Average Directional Index)

- HMA (Hull Moving Average)

  Change HMA length to 50

Strategy Overview:

This strategy is designed to catch large swings in the market using the kNN indicator and HMA for entries/exits. The kNN can produce false signals in sideways markets, so the ADX is used to avoid entering in choppy market conditions.

The 500 EMA is used to trade in the direction of the overall market trend.

Buy/Long Conditions:

- Price is above the 500 EMA

- The ADX is above 25

- Price is above the HMA

- Enter long when a buy signal (blue label) appears from the kNN indicator

- Exit long when a candle closes below the HMA or a sell signal (red label) appears from the kNN indicator

Sell/Short Conditions:

- Price is below the 500 EMA

- The ADX is above 25

- Price is below the HMA

- Enter short when a sell signal (red label) appears from the kNN indicator

- Exit short when a candle closes above the HMA or a buy signal (blue label) appears from the kNN indicator

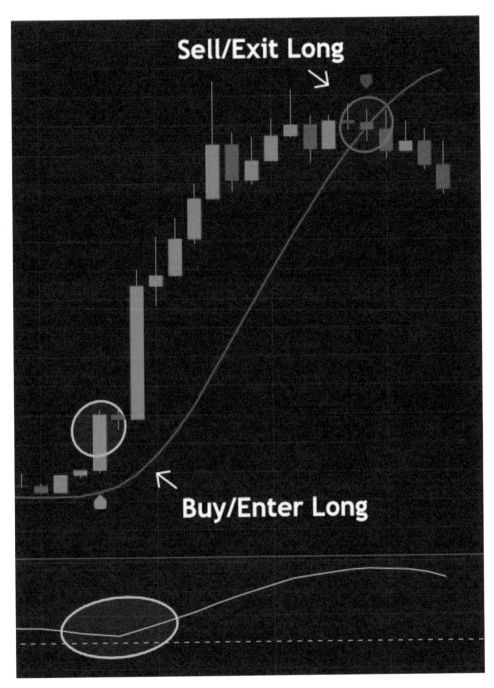

Example of a long entry and exit using this strategy

Scalping Strategy #6: Auto Harmonic Pattern + Wavetrend Strategy

Strategy Indicators:

- 500 EMA

- Wavetrend in Dynamic Zones with Kumo Implied Volatility

- Auto Harmonic Patterns - V2

Strategy Overview:

This strategy uses the Auto Harmonic Patterns (HP) to identify entries/exits and signals from the Wavetrend for confirmation. The HP indicator will generate a signal when it detects a bullish or bearish pattern, when a pattern is detected it will show the price targets and stop loss levels on your chart.

The 500 EMA is used in this strategy to trade in the direction of the overall trend.

Buy/Long Conditions:

- Price is above the 500 EMA

- The wavetrend is in the oversold (blue) zone

- Enter long trade when the HP indicator detects a bullish pattern and the wavetrend generates a buy signal(crosses up). Place stop loss according to the level given by the HP indicator.

- Exit long when price reaches "target 2" on the HP indicator, or a sell signal occurs on the wavetrend indicator

Sell/Short Conditions:

- Price is below the 500 EMA

- The wavetrend is in the overbought (orange) zone

- Enter short trade when the HP indicator detects a bearish pattern and the wavetrend generates a sell signal(crosses down). Place stop loss according to the level given by the HP indicator.

- Exit short when price reaches "target 2" on the HP indicator, or a buy signal occurs on the wavetrend indicator

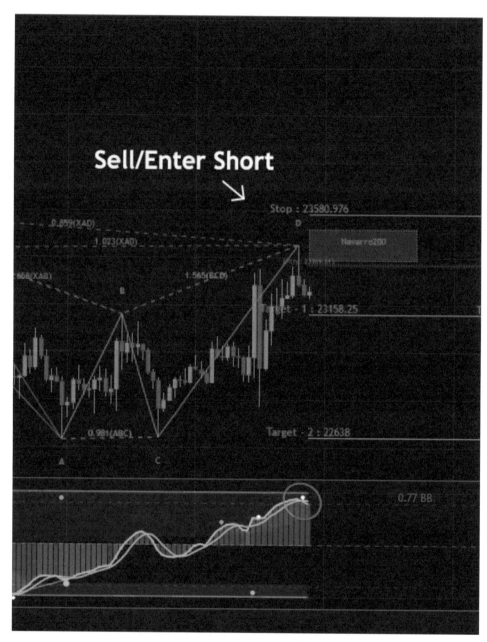

Example of a short entry using this strategy

Chapter 5: Optimizing Your Scalping Strategy to Maximize Profits

Backtesting and Forward Testing Your Strategy

Backtesting involves using historical data to test the effectiveness of your strategy. It helps identify potential weaknesses, allowing you to improve your strategy accordingly. Ensure proper risk management and position sizing during backtesting.

Forward testing involves testing your strategy with real-time data in a simulated trading environment. Monitor performance to identify potential issues and make necessary adjustments. Validate your strategy's effectiveness before using it in a live trading environment.

- Test your strategy using historical data and real-time data in a simulated environment

- Identify weaknesses and make adjustments to improve your strategy

- Validate your strategy's effectiveness before live trading

Adapting to Changing Market Conditions and Regime Shifts

To effectively adapt to changing market conditions and regime shifts, it's crucial to develop a deep understanding of the market environment and be prepared to make adjustments to your strategy as needed. Here are some key areas to focus on:

Monitoring Market Conditions

- Recognizing Regime Shifts

  Identify trending and ranging markets: Recognize when the market is in a strong trend or a consolidation phase, as different strategies may be more effective in different market regimes.

- Understand market cycles: Familiarize yourself with the various phases of market cycles, such as expansion, peak, contraction, and trough, to anticipate potential shifts in market conditions.

- Monitor volatility: Keep an eye on market volatility, as it may indicate potential regime shifts or periods of uncertainty that could require adjustments to your strategy.

Adjusting Your Strategy

- Modify indicator settings: Adjust the settings of your technical indicators to better capture market trends and conditions, such as increasing the lookback period of a moving average during a trending market.

- Adapt entry and exit rules: Tweak your entry and exit rules to suit the prevailing market conditions, such as using a trailing stop-loss order during strong trends or being more selective with entry signals during consolidation periods.

- Adjust risk management: Adapt your risk management strategy to align with changing market conditions. For example, reduce position sizes during periods of increased market volatility or tighten stop-loss orders during strong trends.

Optimizing Indicator Settings

Optimizing indicator settings is crucial to improve the effectiveness of your scalping strategy. By fine-tuning the parameters, you can adapt your strategy to suit your trading style and the current market conditions.

Fine-tuning Indicator Parameters

- Test different parameter values: Experiment with various parameter values for each indicator to determine which settings produce the best results. This process will help you find the most effective settings for your trading strategy and the specific market conditions you're trading in.

- Avoid over-optimization: While it's important to optimize your indicator settings, be cautious of over-optimizing, as it can lead to curve-fitting. Curve-fitting occurs when a strategy is overly tailored to historical data, which can reduce its effectiveness in future market conditions.

- Use out-of-sample testing: To ensure the optimized settings are robust, perform out-of-sample testing by applying the optimized settings to a different data set than what was used for the optimization process. This helps validate the effectiveness of your optimized settings in varying market conditions.

Combining Multiple Indicators

- Diversify your signals: Using multiple indicators can provide you with a more comprehensive view of the market and reduce the likelihood of false signals. By combining indicators, you can filter out noise and increase the accuracy of your entries and exits.

- Optimize the combination of indicators: Just as with individual indicator settings, you can optimize the combination of indicators used in your strategy. Experiment with different combinations of leading and lagging indicators to find the most effective pairing for your specific trading style and market conditions.

- Balance simplicity and effectiveness: While combining multiple indicators can improve the effectiveness of your strategy, it's essential to strike a balance between simplicity and effectiveness. Overcomplicating your strategy with too many indicators can lead to confusion and hinder your decision-making process.

Key Takeaways:

- Fine-tune your indicator settings to adapt to your trading style and market conditions

- Test different parameter values and avoid over-optimization

- Combine multiple indicators to diversify signals and improve the effectiveness of your strategy

- Optimize the combination of indicators and strike a balance between simplicity and effectiveness

Made in the USA
Columbia, SC
05 November 2024

45604634R00054